MW00365187

Contents

Meet the Designer

Mike Vickery has been designing for the cross-stitch industry for over 17 years. He has created designs for many different media, including chart packs, leaflets, magazines and books. He began his cross-stitching career with Color Charts, and then became a free-lance designer working for dozens of magazines and publishers, including *Better Homes and Gardens, Crazy for CrossStitch!, Just Cross Stitch, The Cross Stitcher*, ASN/DRG, Plaid, Leisure Arts and the Needlecraft Shop.

In 1998, he began his own publishing company, Vickery Collection, offering chart packs and kits, including many Celtic designs.

Mike has always been interested in a variety of art subjects, but his early favorites were animals and flowers. In the late 1990s, Mike was commissioned to create a book of Celtic designs. This sparked his continuing fascination with Celtic art. He was intrigued by the way simple motifs were used to create complex designs.

Mike loves the fascinating use of colors, which bring the designs to life. Mike enjoys the challenge of taking classic Celtic design elements, mixed with a contemporary twist, to create a unique design. Though not Irish himself, Mike has a great appreciation for the history of Ireland that is represented in Celtic art.

House of White Birches, Berne, Indiana 46711   AnniesAttic.com

Tara Cross

STITCH COUNT
144 wide x 180 high

APPROXIMATE DESIGN SIZE
11-count 13" x 16⅜"
14-count 10¼" x 12⅞"
16-count 9" x 11¼"
18-count 8" x 10"

CROSS-STITCH (2X)

ANCHOR		DMC	COLORS
73	⟩	151	Very light dusty rose
342	∞	153	Very light violet*
148	⬆	311	Medium navy blue*
162	⊕	517	Dark wedgewood
1038	n	519	Sky blue*
891	△	676	Light old gold
886	Y	677	Very light old gold*
901	⧉	680	Dark old gold
923	●	699	Green*
226	#	702	Kelly green
256	a	704	Bright chartreuse*
304	⋘	741	Medium tangerine
302	6	743	Medium yellow
300	L	745	Light pale yellow
275	·	746	Off-white
218	■	890	Ultra dark pistachio green*
59	◮	3350	Ultra dark dusty rose
75	3	3733	Dusty rose

*And/or Quarter Stitches

BACKSTITCH (1X)

ANCHOR		DMC	COLOR
897	—	902	Very dark garnet

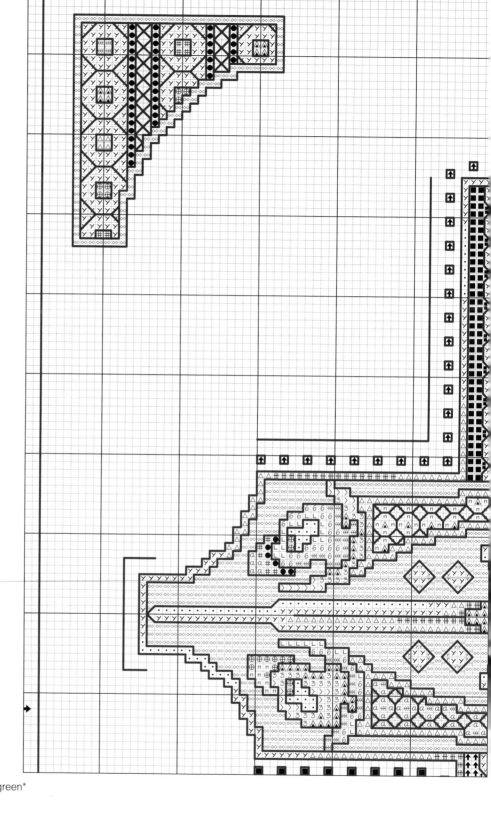

House of White Birches, Berne, Indiana 46711   AnniesAttic.com

CROSS-STITCH (2X)

ANCHOR		DMC	COLORS
73	⟩	151	Very light dusty rose
342	∞	153	Very light violet*
148	↑	311	Medium navy blue*
162	⊕	517	Dark wedgewood
1038	n	519	Sky blue*
891	△	676	Light old gold
886	Y	677	Very light old gold*
901	⊞	680	Dark old gold
923	●	699	Green*
226	#	702	Kelly green
256	a	704	Bright chartreuse*
304	⋘	741	Medium tangerine
302	6	743	Medium yellow
300	L	745	Light pale yellow
275	·	746	Off-white
218	■	890	Ultra dark pistachio green*
59	◭	3350	Ultra dark dusty rose
75	3	3733	Dusty rose

*And/or Quarter Stitches

BACKSTITCH (1X)

ANCHOR		DMC	COLOR
897	▬	902	Very dark garnet

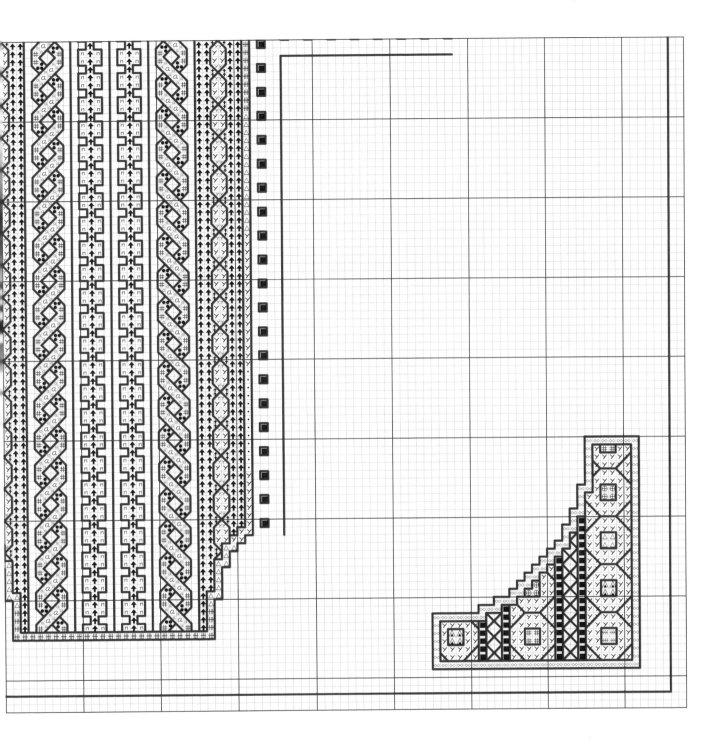

Knots Cross

STITCH COUNT

105 wide x 159 high

APPROXIMATE DESIGN SIZE

11-count 9½" x 14½"
14-count 7½" x 11⅜"
16-count 7½" x 10"
18-count 5⅞" x 8⅞"

CROSS-STITCH (2X)

ANCHOR		DMC	COLORS
120	~	157	Very light cornflower blue
123	●	158	Very dark medium cornflower blue
403	◆	310	Black
59	⊕	600	Very dark cranberry*
63	3	602	Medium cranberry
55	/	604	Light cranberry*
316	#	740	Tangerine
303	8	742	Light tangerine*
301	>	744	Pale yellow*
176	a	793	Medium cornflower blue
274	□	928	Very light gray-green
330	■	947	Burnt orange*
186	6	959	Medium sea green
185	2	964	Light sea green*
188	✖	3812	Very dark sea green*
386	(	3823	Ultra pale yellow
2	·	White	White

*And/or Quarter Stitches

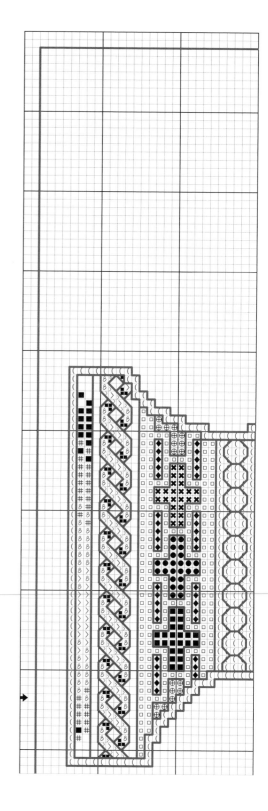

STRIAGHT STITCH (2X)

ANCHOR		DMC	COLOR
333	—	900	Dark burnt orange

BACKSTITCH (1X)

ANCHOR		DMC	COLOR
333	—	900	Dark burnt orange

House of White Birches, Berne, Indiana 46711   AnniesAttic.com

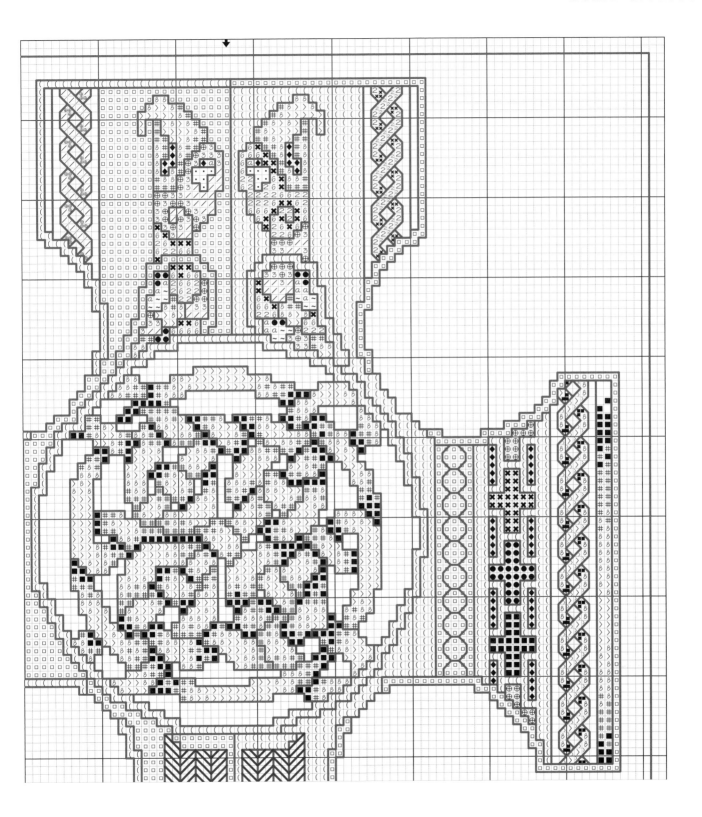

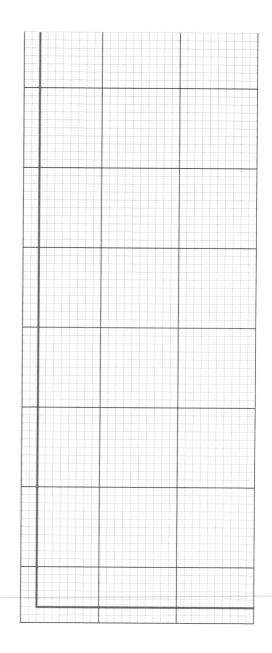

CROSS-STITCH (2X)

ANCHOR		DMC	COLORS
120	~	157	Very light cornflower blue
123	●	158	Very dark medium cornflower blue
403	◆	310	Black
59	⊕	600	Very dark cranberry*
63	3	602	Medium cranberry
55	/	604	Light cranberry*
316	#	740	Tangerine
303	8	742	Light tangerine*
301	>	744	Pale yellow*
176	a	793	Medium cornflower blue
274	□	928	Very light gray-green
330	■	947	Burnt orange*
186	6	959	Medium sea green
185	2	964	Light sea green*
188	✖	3812	Very dark sea green*
386	(	3823	Ultra pale yellow
2	·	White	White

*And/or Quarter Stitches

STRIAGHT STITCH (2X)

ANCHOR		DMC	COLOR
333	—	900	Dark burnt orange

BACKSTITCH (1X)

ANCHOR		DMC	COLOR
333	—	900	Dark burnt orange

House of White Birches, Berne, Indiana 46711   AnniesAttic.com

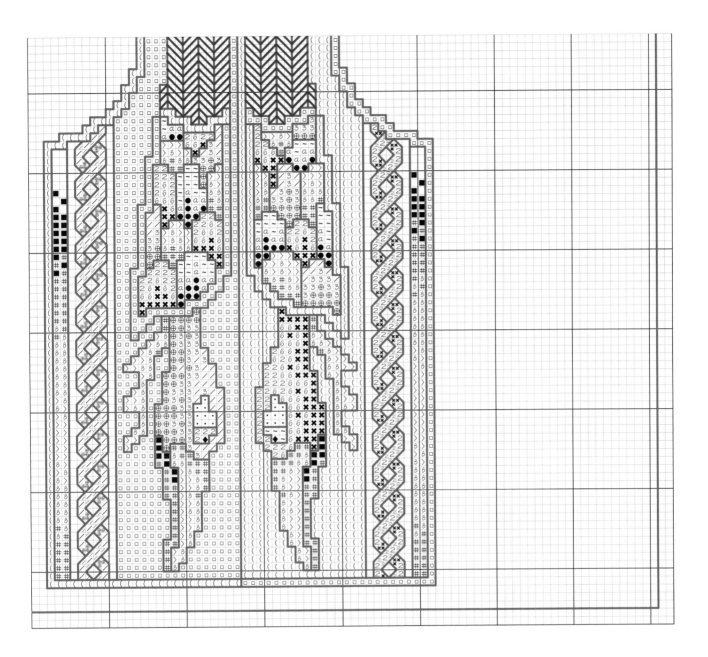

Iona Cross

STITCH COUNT

138 wide x 174 high

APPROXIMATE DESIGN SIZE

11-count 12½" x 15⅞"
14-count 9⅞" x 12⅜"
16-count 8⅝" x 10⅞"
18-count 7⅝" x 9⅝"

CROSS-STITCH (2X)

ANCHOR		DMC	COLORS
109	/	209	Dark lavender
978	?	322	Dark baby blue
858	‹‹‹	524	Very light fern green
102	◆	550	Very dark violet
99	#	552	Medium violet
891	⌐	676	Light old gold
886	⌐	677	Very light old gold
305	⊞	725	Medium light topaz
293	Y	727	Very light topaz
890	⌘	729	Medium old gold
306	✖	783	Medium topaz
43	✿	815	Medium garnet
229	↑	910	Dark emerald green
209	△	912	Light emerald green
204	~	913	Medium Nile green
881	ƍ	945	Tawny
140	a	3755	Baby blue
875	c	3813	Light blue-green
901	▼	3829	Very dark old gold
2	·	White	White

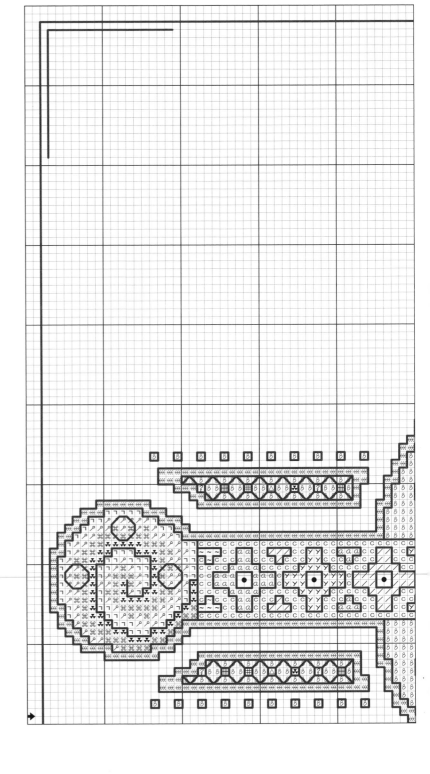

BACKSTITCH (1X)

ANCHOR		DMC	COLOR
43	▬	815	Medium garnet

FRENCH KNOT (1X)

ANCHOR		DMC	COLOR
43	●	815	Medium garnet

House of White Birches, Berne, Indiana 46711   AnniesAttic.com

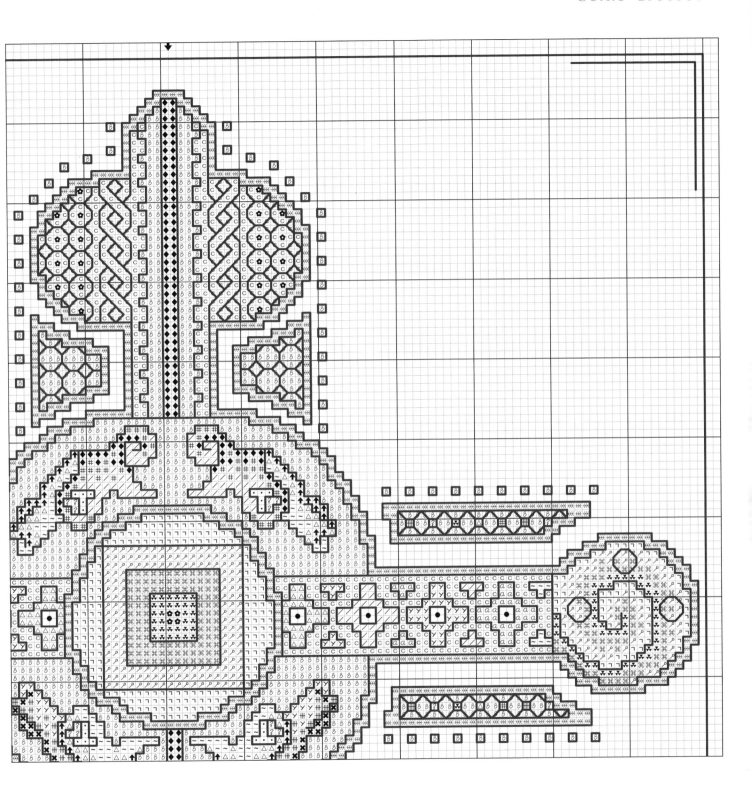

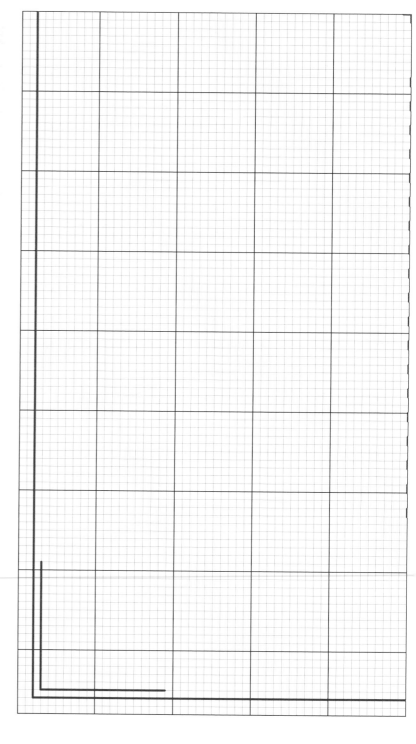

CROSS-STITCH (2X)

ANCHOR		DMC	COLORS
109	/	209	Dark lavender
978	?	322	Dark baby blue
858	≪	524	Very light fern green
102	◆	550	Very dark violet
99	#	552	Medium violet
891	⌐	676	Light old gold
886	⌐	677	Very light old gold
305	⧻	725	Medium light topaz
293	Y	727	Very light topaz
890	⌘	729	Medium old gold
306	✖	783	Medium topaz
43	✿	815	Medium garnet
229	↑	910	Dark emerald green
209	△	912	Light emerald green
204	~	913	Medium Nile green
881	8	945	Tawny
140	a	3755	Baby blue
875	c	3813	Light blue-green
901	✦	3829	Very dark old gold
2	·	White	White

BACKSTITCH (1X)

ANCHOR		DMC	COLOR
43	▬	815	Medium garnet

FRENCH KNOT (1X)

ANCHOR		DMC	COLOR
43	●	815	Medium garnet

House of White Birches, Berne, Indiana 46711   AnniesAttic.com

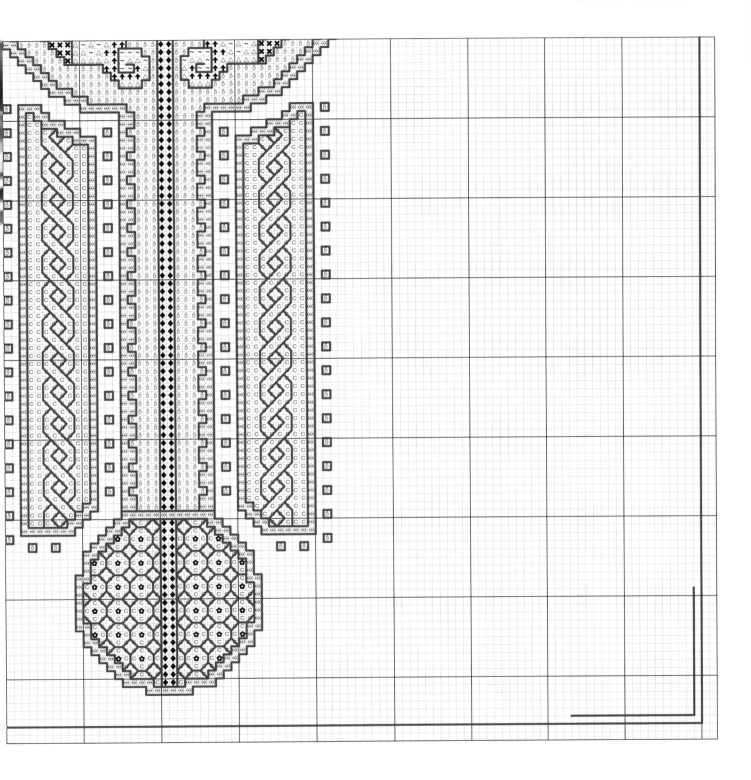

Mini Cross

STITCH COUNT
56 wide x 80 high

APPROXIMATE DESIGN SIZE
11-count 5" x 7¼"
14-count 4" x 5¾"
16-count 3½" x 5"
18-count 3⅛" x 4⅜"

CROSS-STITCH (2X)

ANCHOR		DMC	COLORS
293	e	165	Very light moss green*
150	↑	336	Navy blue
117	o	341	Light blue-violet*
162	⊕	517	Medium dark wedgewood*
1039	#	518	Light wedgewood
1038	/	519	Sky blue*
1062	△	598	Light turquoise*
259	(	772	Very light yellow-green*
923	▲	909	Very dark emerald green*
205	≪	911	Medium emerald green
204	>	913	Medium Nile green*
274	~	928	Very light gray-green*
185	m	964	Light sea green*
1032	L	3752	Very light antique blue*
875	6	3817	Light celadon green*

*And/or Quarter Stitches

BACKSTITCH (1X)

ANCHOR		DMC	COLOR
152	▬	939	Very dark navy blue

House of White Birches, Berne, Indiana 46711 AnniesAttic.com

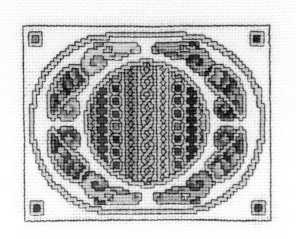

Mini Medallion

STITCH COUNT

80 wide x 60 high

APPROXIMATE DESIGN SIZE

11-count 7¼" x 5½"
14-count 5¾" x 4¼"
16-count 5" x 3¾"
18-count 4½" x 3⅜"

CROSS-STITCH (2X)

ANCHOR		DMC	COLORS
73	~	151	Very light dusty rose
109	⊕	155	Medium dark blue-violet
119	▼	333	Very dark blue-violet
117	⟩	341	Light blue-violet
886	△	677	Very light old gold
305	Y	725	Medium light topaz
293	/	727	Very light topaz
306	↑	783	Medium topaz
229	X	910	Dark emerald green
209	⫸	912	Light emerald green
203	○	954	Nile green
59	♥	3350	Ultra dark dusty rose
75	ß	3733	Dusty rose
1031	m	3753	Ultra very light antique blue

BACKSTITCH (1X)

ANCHOR		DMC	COLOR
268	—	3345	Dark hunter green

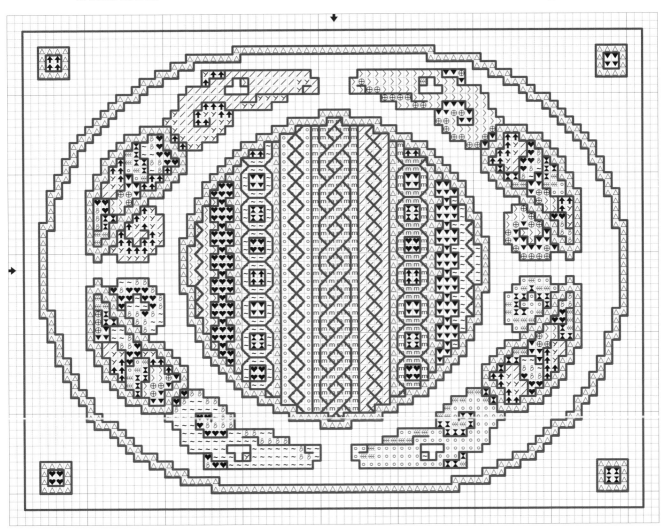

MacRegol Medallion

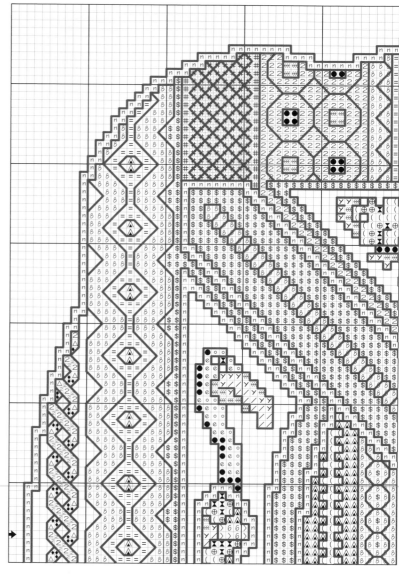

STITCH COUNT

129 wide x 129 high

APPROXIMATE DESIGN SIZE

11-count 11¾" x 11¾"
14-count 9¼" x 9¼"
16-count 8" x 8"
18-count 7⅛" x 7⅛"

CROSS-STITCH (2X)

ANCHOR		DMC	COLORS
342	o	153	Very light violet
1006	△	304	Medium red
117	=	341	Light blue-violet
99	●	552	Medium violet
96	e	554	Light violet
46	6	666	Bright red
891	a	676	Light old gold
886	n	677	Very light old gold
901	■	680	Dark old gold
305	Y	725	Medium light topaz
293	/	727	Very light topaz
—	⊮	728	Topaz
275	L	746	Off-white
259	2	772	Very light yellow-green*
1044	◆	895	Very dark hunter green*
848	#	927	Light gray-green
186	⊕	959	Medium sea green
185	(	964	Light sea green
267	△	3346	Hunter green*
35	>	3705	Dark melon
188	✕	3812	Very dark sea green
1076	$	3847	Dark teal-green
311	ଃ	3855	Light autumn gold

*And/or Quarter Stitches

STRAIGHT STITCH (2X)

ANCHOR		DMC	COLOR
352	—	300	Very dark mahogany

BACKSTITCH (1X)

ANCHOR		DMC	COLOR
352	—	300	Very dark mahogany

House of White Birches, Berne, Indiana 46711   AnniesAttic.com

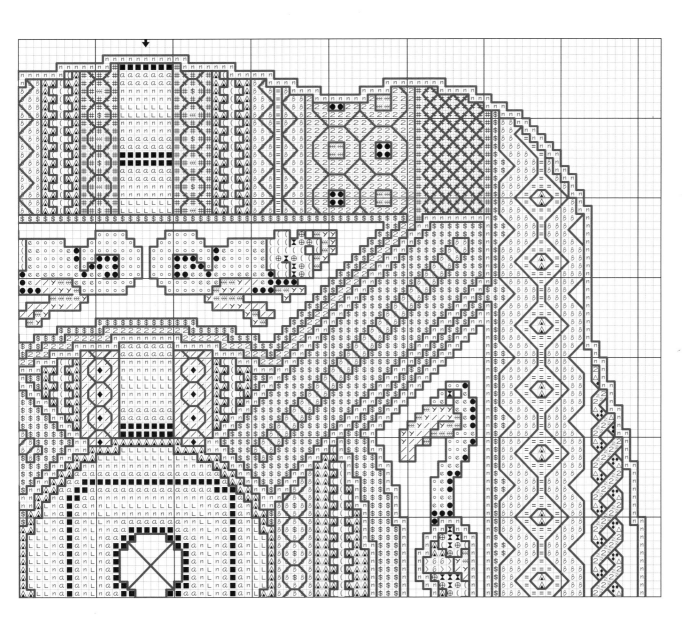

CROSS-STITCH (2X)

ANCHOR		DMC	COLORS
342	o	153	Very light violet
1006	△	304	Medium red
117	=	341	Light blue-violet
99	●	552	Medium violet
96	e	554	Light violet
46	6	666	Bright red
891	a	676	Light old gold
886	n	677	Very light old gold
901	■	680	Dark old gold
305	Y	725	Medium light topaz
293	/	727	Very light topaz
—	≪	728	Topaz
275	L	746	Off-white
259	2	772	Very light yellow-green*
1044	◆	895	Very dark hunter green*
848	#	927	Light gray-green
186	⊕	959	Medium sea green
185	(	964	Light sea green
267	△	3346	Hunter green*
35	>	3705	Dark melon
188	✕	3812	Very dark sea green
1076	$	3847	Dark teal-green
311	8	3855	Light autumn gold

*And/or Quarter Stitches

STRAIGHT STITCH (2X)

ANCHOR		DMC	COLOR
352	▬	300	Very dark mahogany

BACKSTITCH (1X)

ANCHOR		DMC	COLOR
352	▬	300	Very dark mahogany

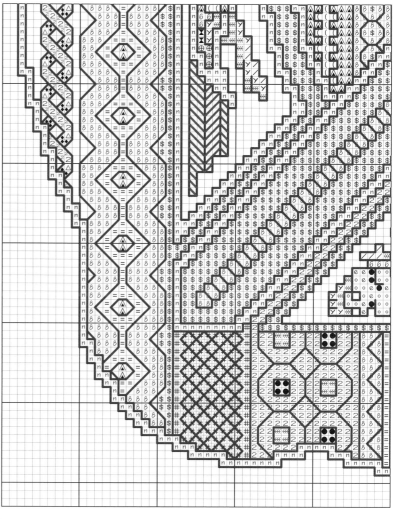

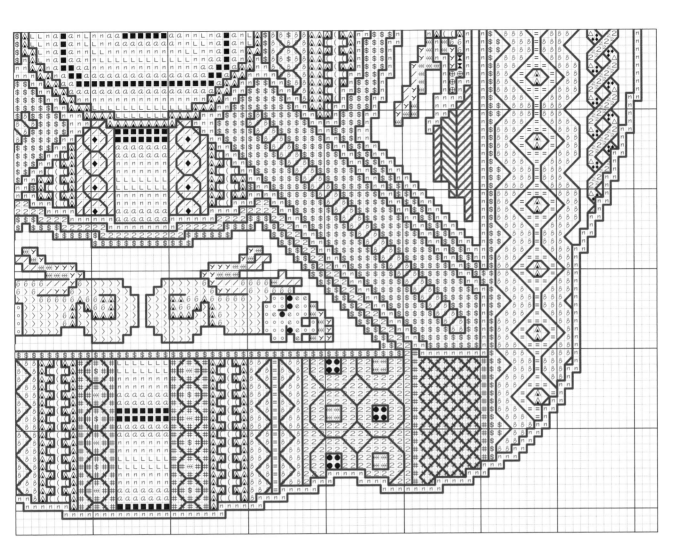

Durrow Medallion

STITCH COUNT
130 wide x 128 high

APPROXIMATE DESIGN SIZE
11-count 11⅞" x 11⅝"
14-count 9¼" x 9⅛"
16-count 8⅛" x 8"
18-count 7¼" x 7"

CROSS-STITCH (2X)

ANCHOR		DMC	COLORS
73	L	151	Very light dusty rose
342	/	153	Very light violet
1006	↑	304	Medium red
99	◿	552	Medium violet
96	枀	554	Light violet
46	6	666	Bright red
886	⌗	677	Very light old gold
305	Y	725	Medium light topaz
293	(	727	Very light topaz
158	>	747	Very light sky blue
306	✗	783	Medium topaz
131	▲	798	Dark delft blue
168	⌘	807	Peacock blue
130	3	809	Delft blue
134	■	820	Very dark royal blue
874	△	834	Very light golden-olive
923	✻	909	Very dark emerald green
205	⋘	911	Medium emerald green
204	a	913	Medium Nile green
59	◆	3350	Ultra dark dusty rose
35	n	3705	Dark melon
75	⊕	3733	Dusty rose
170	♣	3765	Very dark peacock blue
167	⧻	3766	Light peacock blue

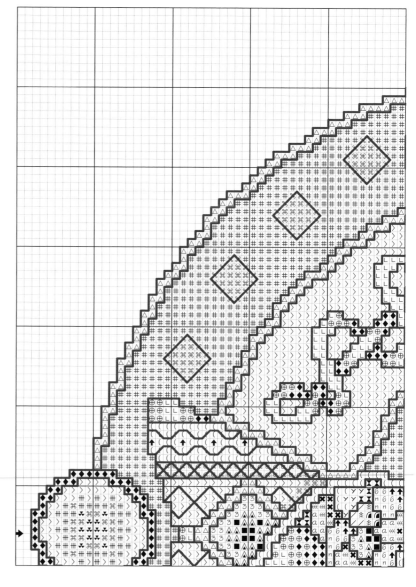

BACKSTITCH (1X)

ANCHOR	DMC	COLOR
897	— 902	Very dark garnet

House of White Birches, Berne, Indiana 46711   AnniesAttic.com

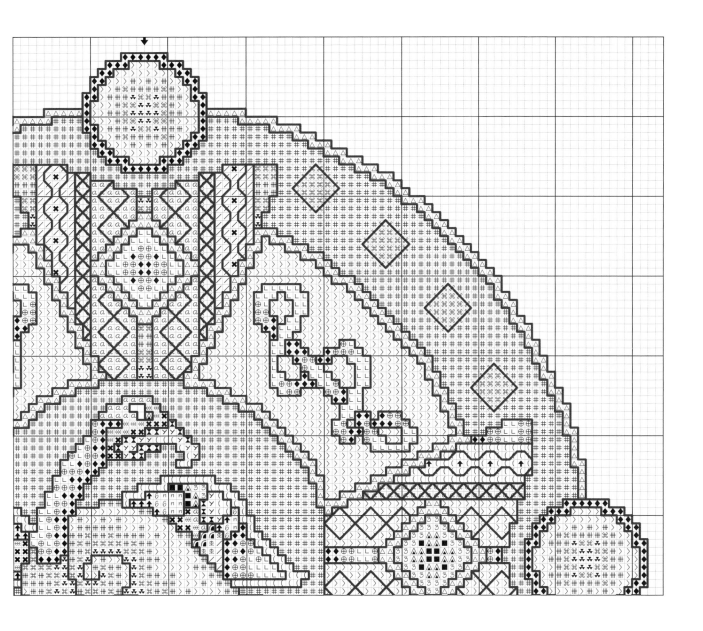

CROSS-STITCH (2X)

ANCHOR		DMC	COLORS
73	L	151	Very light dusty rose
342	/	153	Very light violet
1006	↑	304	Medium red
99	◪	552	Medium violet
96	余	554	Light violet
46	6	666	Bright red
886	#	677	Very light old gold
305	Y	725	Medium light topaz
293	(	727	Very light topaz
158	>	747	Very light sky blue
306	I	783	Medium topaz
131	▲	798	Dark delft blue
168	⌘	807	Peacock blue
130	3	809	Delft blue
134	■	820	Very dark royal blue
874	△	834	Very light golden-olive
923	✖	909	Very dark emerald green
205	⋘	911	Medium emerald green
204	a	913	Medium Nile green
59	◆	3350	Ultra dark dusty rose
35	n	3705	Dark melon
75	⊕	3733	Dusty rose
170	⤓	3765	Very dark peacock blue
167	⌗	3766	Light peacock blue

BACKSTITCH (1X)

ANCHOR		DMC	COLOR
897	—	902	Very dark garnet

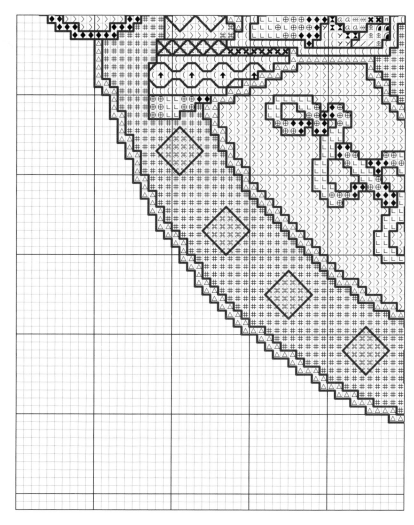

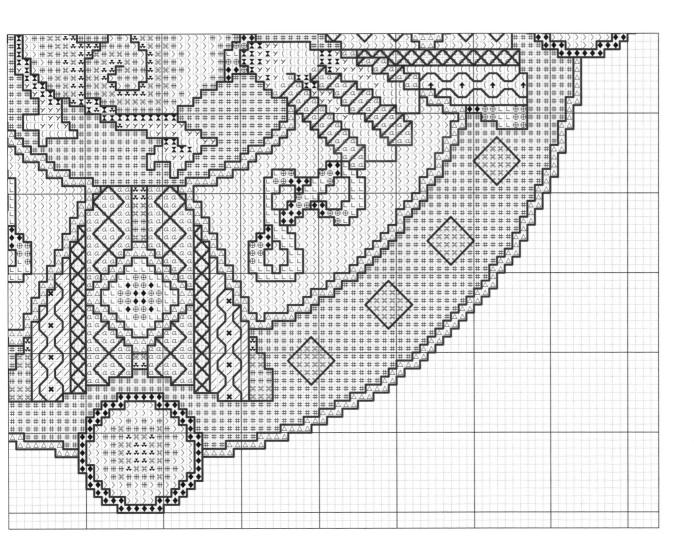

2/16/12 - diamonds were all stitched using
DMC 912 Lt Emerald Green - this was a mistake
They should have been done in DMC 815 med garnet

Newton Column

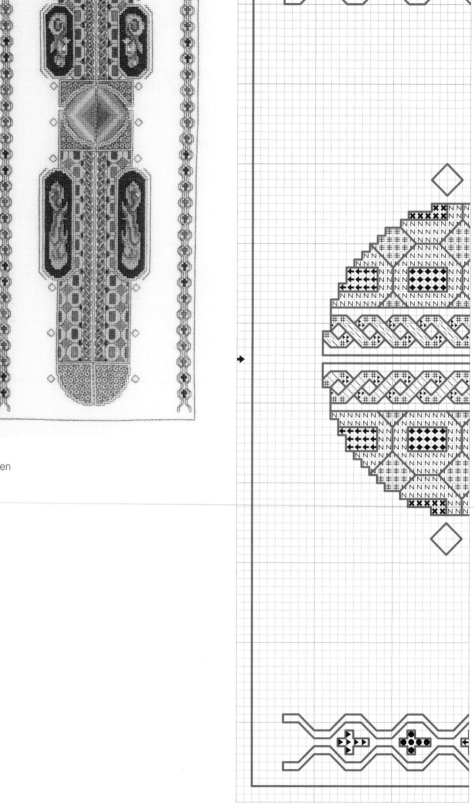

STITCH COUNT
107 wide x 242 high

APPROXIMATE DESIGN SIZE
11-count 9¾" x 22"
14-count 7⅝" x 17¼"
16-count 6⅝" x 15⅛"
18-count 5⅞" x 13⅜"

CROSS-STITCH (2X)

ANCHOR		DMC	COLORS
293	~	165	Very light moss green
279	⌘	166	Medium light moss green
118	6	340	Medium blue-violet
117	△	341	Light blue-violet
280	●	581	Moss green
1064	3	597	Turquoise
886	e	677	Very light old gold
43	⊞	815	Medium garnet
277	◆	831	Medium golden-olive
907	Y	833	Light golden-olive
874	>	834	Very light golden-olive
229	▼	910	Dark emerald green*
209	#	912	Light emerald green
274	Z	928	Very light gray-green
203	/	954	Nile green*
246	◭	986	Very dark forest green
1030	✖	3746	Dark blue-violet
1066	♠	3809	Very dark turquoise
1060	n	3811	Very light turquoise
2	·	White	White

*And/or Quarter Stitches

BACKSTITCH (1X)

ANCHOR		DMC	COLOR
1076	—	3847	Dark teal-green

House of White Birches, Berne, Indiana 46711 AnniesAttic.com

e green diamonds will need to be photoshopped
as OMC 815 med. garnet for page 24 and back cover. Celtic Crosses
Marla has this change.

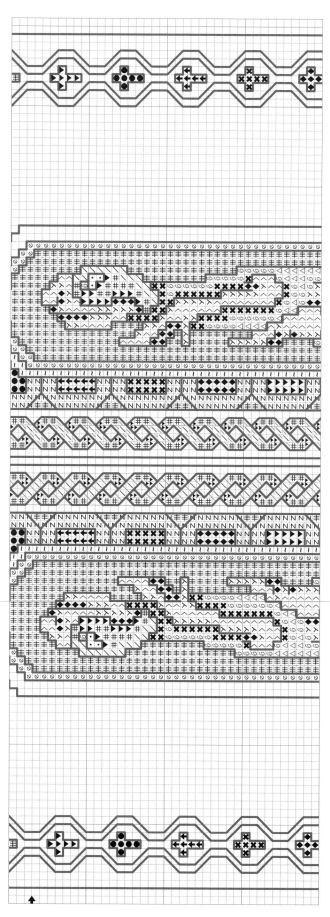

CROSS-STITCH (2X)

ANCHOR		DMC	COLORS
293	~	165	Very light moss green
279	⌘	166	Medium light moss green
118	6	340	Medium blue-violet
117	△	341	Light blue-violet
280	●	581	Moss green
1064	3	597	Turquoise
886	e	677	Very light old gold
43	⧻	815	Medium garnet
277	◆	831	Medium golden-olive
907	Y	833	Light golden-olive
874	>	834	Very light golden-olive
229	▼	910	Dark emerald green*
209	#	912	Light emerald green
274	Z	928	Very light gray-green
203	/	954	Nile green*
246	◮	986	Very dark forest green
1030	✖	3746	Dark blue-violet
1066	↑	3809	Very dark turquoise
1060	n	3811	Very light turquoise
2	·	White	White

*And/or Quarter Stitches

BACKSTITCH (1X)

ANCHOR		DMC	COLOR
1076	—	3847	Dark teal-green

House of White Birches, Berne, Indiana 46711   AnniesAttic.com

Evangeli Column

STITCH COUNT
50 wide x 280 high

APPROXIMATE DESIGN SIZE
11-count 4½" x 25½"
14-count 3½" x 20"
16-count 3⅛" x 17½"
18-count 2¾" x 15½"

CROSS-STITCH (2X)

ANCHOR		DMC	COLORS
109	n	209	Dark lavender
342	/	211	Light lavender
1038	3	519	Sky blue
212	⊥	561	Very dark jade
886	e	677	Very light old gold
45	⌘	814	Dark garnet
9159	(	828	Ultra very light blue
25	<	3716	Very light dusty rose
169	↑	3760	Medium wedgewood
876	⊕	3816	Medium celadon green
875	o	3817	Light celadon green
305	⊞	3821	Straw
295	△	3822	Light straw
29	✕	3831	Dark raspberry
26	⋘	3833	Light raspberry
100	▼	3837	Ultra dark lavender
306	◭	3852	Very dark straw

BACKSTITCH (1X)

ANCHOR		DMC	COLOR
873	—	154	Very dark grape

House of White Birches, Berne, Indiana 46711   AnniesAttic.com

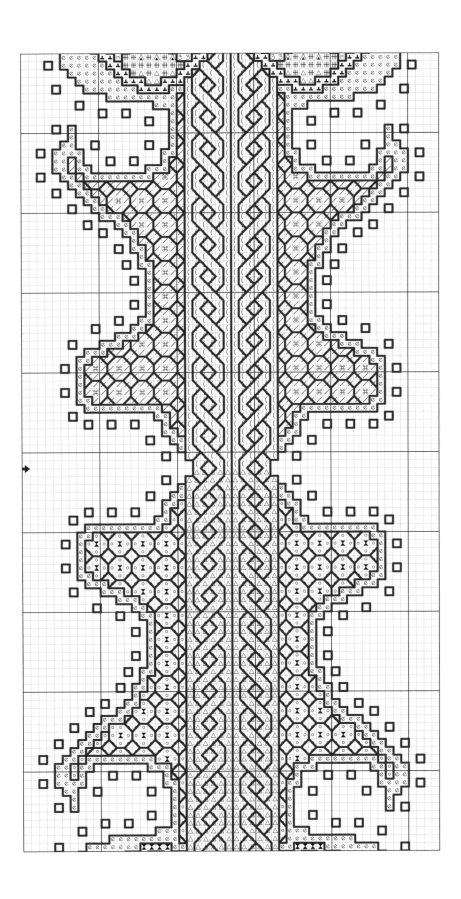

CROSS-STITCH (2X)

ANCHOR		DMC	COLORS
109	n	209	Dark lavender
342	/	211	Light lavender
1038	3	519	Sky blue
212	⊥	561	Very dark jade
886	e	677	Very light old gold
45	⌘	814	Dark garnet
9159	(	828	Ultra very light blue
25	<	3716	Very light dusty rose
169	↑	3760	Medium wedgewood
876	⊕	3816	Medium celadon green
875	o	3817	Light celadon green
305	⊞	3821	Straw
295	△	3822	Light straw
29	⊠	3831	Dark raspberry
26	⋘	3833	Light raspberry
100	▼	3837	Ultra dark lavender
306	◮	3852	Very dark straw

BACKSTITCH (1X)

ANCHOR		DMC	COLOR
873	—	154	Very dark grape

How to Stitch

Working From Charted Designs

A square on a chart corresponds to a space for a Cross-Stitch on the stitching surface. The symbol in a square shows the floss color to be used for the stitch. The width and height for the design stitch-area are given; centers are shown by arrows. Backstitches, Straight Stitches and Running Stitches are shown by straight lines, and French Knots by dots.

Fabrics

Our cover models were worked on white 18-count Davosa by Zweigart. Davosa is an even-weave fabric that has the same number of horizontal and vertical threads (or blocks of threads) per inch. That number is called the thread count.

The size of the design is determined by the size of the even-weave fabric on which you work. Use the chart below as a guide to determine the finished size of a design on various popular sizes of Aida cloth.

Thread Count	Number of Stitches in Design				
	10	20	30	40	50
11-count	1"	1¾"	2¾"	3⅝"	4½"
14-count	¾"	1⅜"	2⅛"	2⅞"	3⅝"
16-count	⅝"	1¼"	1⅞"	2½"	3⅛"
18-count	½"	1⅛"	1⅝"	2¼"	2¾"

(measurements are given to the nearest ⅛")

Needles

A blunt-tipped tapestry needle, size 24 or 26, is used for stitching on 14-count fabrics. The higher the needle number, the smaller the needle. The correct size needle is easy to thread with the amount of floss required, but is not so large that it will distort the holes in the fabric. The following chart indicates the appropriate size needle for each size of fabric, along with the suggested number of strands of floss to use.

Fabric	Stitches Per Inch	Strands of Floss	Tapestry Needle Size
Aida	11	3	22 or 24
Aida	14	2	24 or 26
Aida	16	2	24, 26 or 28
Aida	18	2	26 or 28

Floss

Our cover models were stitched with DMC 6-strand embroidery floss. Anchor floss numbers are also listed. The companies have different color ranges, so these are only suggested substitutions. Floss color names are given. Cut floss into comfortable working lengths; we suggest about 18 inches.

Getting Started

To begin in an unstitched area, bring threaded needle from back to front of fabric. Hold an inch of the end against the back, and then hold it in place with your first few stitches. To end threads and begin new ones next to existing stitches, weave through the backs of several stitches.

The Stitches

Use two strands of floss for all Cross-Stitches and Quarter Stitches, and one strand for Backstitches, Straight Stitches and French Knots, unless otherwise noted in the color key.

Cross-Stitch

The Cross-Stitch is formed in two motions. Follow the numbering in Fig. 1 and bring needle up at 1, down at 2, up at 3, down at 4, to complete the stitch. Work horizontal rows of stitches (Fig. 2) wherever possible. Bring thread up at 1, work half of each stitch across the row, and then complete the stitches on your return.

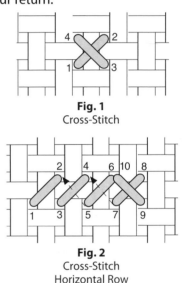

Fig. 1
Cross-Stitch

Fig. 2
Cross-Stitch
Horizontal Row

Quarter Stitch

The Quarter Stitch is formed in one motion. Follow the numbering in Fig. 3 and bring needle up at 1 and down at 2. The Quarter Stitch is used to fill in small spaces in the design where there is not enough room for a full stitch.

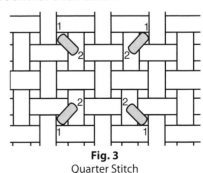

Fig. 3
Quarter Stitch

Backstitch

Backstitches are worked after Cross-Stitches have been completed. They may slope in any direction and are occasionally worked over more than one square of fabric. Fig. 4 shows the progression of several stitches; bring thread up at odd numbers and down at even numbers. Frequently you must choose where to end one Backstitch color and begin the next color. Choose the object that should appear closest to you. Backstitch around that shape with the appropriate color, and then Backstitch the areas behind it with adjacent color(s).

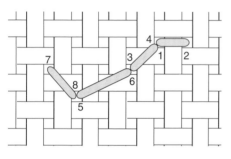

Fig. 4
Backstitch

French Knot

Bring thread up where indicated on chart. Wrap floss once around needle (Fig. 5) and reinsert needle at 2, close to 1, but at least one fabric thread away from it. Hold wrapping thread tightly and pull needle through, letting thread go just as knot is formed. For a larger knot, use more strands of floss.

Fig. 5
French Knot

Planning a Project

If you are working on a piece of fabric, determine the stitched size, and then allow enough additional fabric around the design plus 3 inches more on each side for use in finishing and mounting.

Cut your fabric exactly true, right along the holes of the fabric. Some raveling may occur as you handle the fabric. To minimize raveling along the raw edges, use an overcast basting stitch, machine zigzag stitch or masking tape, which you can cut away when you are finished.

Finishing Needlework

When you have finished stitching, dampen your embroidery (or, if soiled, wash in lukewarm mild soapsuds and rinse well). Roll in a towel to remove excess moisture. Place facedown on a dry towel or padded surface, and press carefully until dry and smooth. Make sure all thread ends are well anchored and clipped closely. Proceed with desired finishing. ■

E-mail: Customer_Service@whitebirches.com

HOUSE of WHITE BIRCHES
PUBLISHERS SINCE 1947

Celtic Crosses is published by DRG, 306 East Parr Road, Berne, IN 46711, telephone (260) 589-4000. Printed in USA. Copyright © 2010 DRG. All rights reserved. This publication may not be reproduced in part or in whole without written permission from the publisher. **RETAIL STORES:** If you would like to carry this pattern book or any other DRG publications, call the Wholesale Department at Annie's Attic to set up a direct account: (903) 636-4303. Also, request a complete listing of publications available from DRG.

Every effort has been made to ensure that the instructions in this pattern book are complete and accurate. We cannot, however, take responsibility for human error, typographical mistakes or variations in individual work.

STAFF

Editor: Barb Sprunger
Technical Editor: Marla Laux
Copy Supervisor: Michelle Beck
Copy Editor: Amanda Scheerer
Graphic Arts Supervisor: Erin Augsburger
Graphic Artists: Glenda Chamberlain, Edith Teegarden

Art Director: Brad Snow
Assistant Art Director: Nick Pierce
Photography Supervisor: Tammy Christian
Photography: Matthew Owen
Photo Stylist: Tammy Steiner

ISBN: 978-1-59012-228-0

1 2 3 4 5 6 7 8 9